Where The Truth Lies

A Play by

Catherine Butterfield

SAMUEL FRENCH, INC.
45 WEST 25TH STREET   NEW YORK 10010
7623 SUNSET BOULEVARD   HOLLYWOOD 90046
LONDON   *TORONTO*

Copyright © 1997 by Catherine Butterfield

ALL RIGHTS RESERVED

CAUTION: Professionals and amateurs are hereby warned that WHERE THE TRUTH LIES is subject to a royalty. It is fully protected under the copyright laws of the United States of America, the British Commonwealth, including Canada, and all other countries of the Copyright Union. All rights, including professional, amateur, motion pictures, recitation, lecturing, public reading, radio broadcasting, television, and the rights of translation into foreign languages are strictly reserved. In its present form the play is dedicated to the reading public only.

The amateur live stage performance rights to WHERE THE TRUTH LIES are controlled exclusively by Samuel French, Inc. and royalty arrangements and licenses must be secured well in advance of presentation. PLEASE NOTE that amateur royalty fees are set upon application in accordance with your producing circumstances. When applying for a royalty quotation and license please give us the number of performances intended, dates of production, your seating capacity and admission fee. Royalties are payable one week before the opening performance of the play to Samuel French, Inc., at 45 W. 25th Street, New York, NY 10010; or at 7623 Sunset Blvd., Hollywood, CA 90046, or to Samuel French (Canada), Ltd., 100 Lombard Street, Toronto, Ontario, Canada M5C 1M3.

Royalty of the required amount must be paid whether the play is presented for charity or gain and whether or not admission is charged.

Stock royalty quoted on application to Samuel French, Inc.

For all other rights than those stipulated above, apply to International Creative Management, Attn.: Sarah J. Leigh, 40 W. 57th Street, New York, NY 10019.

Particular emphasis is laid on the question of amateur or professional readings, permission and terms for which must be secured in writing from Samuel French, Inc.

Copying from this book in whole or in part is strictly forbidden by law, and the right of performance is not transferable.

Whenever the play is produced the following notice must appear on all programs, printing and advertising for the play: "Produced by special arrangement with Samuel French, Inc."

Due authorship credit must be given on all programs, printing and advertising for the play.

ISBN 0 573 66036 0   Printed in U.S.A.   # 25706

No one shall commit or authorize any act or omission by which the copyright of, or the right to copyright, this play may be impaired.

No one shall make any changes in this play for the purpose of production.

Publication of this play does not imply availability for performance. Both amateurs and professionals considering a production are *strongly* advised in their own interests to apply to Samuel French, Inc., for written permission before starting rehearsals, advertising, or booking a theatre.

No part of this book may be reproduced, stored in a retrieval system, or transmitted in any form, by any means, now known or yet to be invented, including mechanical, electronic, photocopying, recording, videotaping, or otherwise, without the prior written permission of the publisher.

IMPORTANT BILLING AND CREDIT REQUIREMENTS

All producers of WHERE THE TRUTH LIES *must* give credit to the Author of the Play in all programs distributed in connection with performances of the Play and in all instances in which the title of the Play appears for purposes of advertising, publicizing or otherwise exploiting the Play and/or a production. The name of the Author *must* also appear on a separate line, on which no other name appears, immediately following the title, and *must* appear in size of type not less than fifty percent the size of the title type.

IRISH REPERTORY THEATRE

WEISSBERGER THEATER GROUP
JAY HARRIS, Producer

Presents

WHERE THE TRUTH LIES
by
CATHERINE BUTTERFIELD

Directed by EVAN YIONOULIS

Set Design	–	DAVID GALLO
Costume Design	–	TERESA SNIDER-STEIN
Lighting Design	–	CHRIS DALLOS
Sound Design	–	JANET KALAS
Production Stage Manager	–	JANA LLYNN
Casting Director	–	MATTHEW MESSINGER
Press Representatives	–	SPRINGER ASSOCIATES
General Management	–	BONA DEA PRODUCTIONS
Executive Producer	–	KATY BOLGER

CAST
(in order of appearance)

Elaine Flanagan	CATHERINE BUTTERFIELD
Wendy Flanagan	BRITTANY BOYD
Leslie Camden	ELLEN DOLAN
Cinda Camden	MISCHA BARTON
Melissa Flanagan	TAYLOR STANLEY
Dan Flanagan	MICHAEL COUNTRYMAN
Vic Camden	ARMAND SCHULTZ

ACT I

Scene One

(A house in a small town in Vermont. The woodwork is dark, the furnishings eclectic but homey. The front door has a stained glass window. A stairway leads from the small vestibule upstairs. The living room occupies the largest part of the set. Flowers are neatly placed in vases all over the house, which is pristine clean. It is summer. At rise, the stage is empty. Then ELAINE FLANAGAN, carrying a laundry hamper, comes down the stairs. She is 37, slightly pretty, and at the moment in a state of nervous tension.)

ELAINE. Melissa, did you give me all your laundry?
MELISSA. *(Off)* Yes!
ELAINE. Okay. I don't want to come upstairs and find a pile of clothing behind your bedroom door, do you hear me? *(Pause)* Do you hear me, Melissa?
MELISSA. *(Off)* Yes! Jesus!
ELAINE. What did you say, young lady?
MELISSA. *(Off)* I said I gave you all my laundry. Take a chill pill.

(ELAINE continues with the laundry through a swinging door leading to the kitchen and laundry room, off. WENDY,

10, enters through the front door. She throws her books down on the table by the door.)

WENDY. Mom, I'm home! Are they here yet? Mom! *(Off)* Mom!
ELAINE. *(Off)* Oh Wendy, good, you're home.
WENDY. *(Off)* Are they here yet?
ELAINE. *(Off)* No. Do I have all your laundry?
WENDY. *(Off)* I gave it to you last night.

(They both re-enter.)

ELAINE. Nothing molding under a dresser?
WENDY. Nope.
ELAINE. Well, your room looked very nice. Thank you for cleaning it up. The living room looks nice, doesn't it?
WENDY. Uh-huh. *(She goes to a bowl on the mantle)* What's this stuff?
ELAINE. Potpourri. To make everything smell pretty.
WENDY. Then what are the flowers for?
ELAINE. Do you think it's too much? Does the room smell too strong?
WENDY. It's fine, Mom. Don't worry about it.
ELAINE. I'm not worried. I'm actually quite calm. Which is a good thing, because your Aunt Leslie hates it when I fuss. *(Pause)* Honey, your hair's a mess. Come here and let me fix it.

(WENDY crosses to her and ELAINE fixes her hair.)

WENDY. When do they get here?

WHERE THE TRUTH LIES 7

ELAINE. Their flight got in 45 minutes ago, so they should be here soon. I don't know why she wouldn't let me pick her up.

WENDY. They're probably gonna take a limousine. Probably a stretch limousine, with a TV and a phone in it.

ELAINE. *(Doubtfully)* Oh, I don't know. That would look awfully silly in this neighborhood. *(Laughing)* What would everyone say if they saw a stretch limo pulling up in front of this house?

WENDY. It would be so cool. Cinda's such a lucky duck, to be that rich.

ELAINE. I'm sure she has her complaints, just like any other little girl.

WENDY. Yeah – "Oh, bummer, the chauffeur is late with the limo. How will I get to the U-2 concert on time?"

ELAINE. I'm sure Cinda isn't going to any rock concerts at her age.

WENDY. *(Exasperated)* Mom! Get real. She's been going to concerts since she was eight.

ELAINE. Oh Wendy, please.

WENDY. She does! Uncle Vic takes her.

ELAINE. At eleven years old? I seriously doubt it.

WENDY. You are so out of it, Mom.

ELAINE. Look, is that them? I think it is! Melissa. Missy!

WENDY. *(Disappointed)* Oh boring, a rental car.

ELAINE. *(Calling upstairs)* Melissa, they're here, come downstairs. *(Going to the door, she sees the pile of books on the table)* Oh, for goodness sake. Wendy, get rid of these books.

WENDY. Where?

ELAINE. Anywhere, just stow them, quickly. Melissa! *(WENDY grabs the books and stashes them. ELAINE opens the front door and waves)* Hi, there! *(To WENDY)* Go help your cousin with her bag. *(WENDY goes outside)* Hi, there, strangers! *(She goes out herself. There is an exclamation of female affection)* Good heavens! Cinda, look at you, you've grown so much, I hardly recognized you. Wendy, take that bag, will you?

CINDA. *(Off)* That's okay. I got it.

ELAINE. *(Off)* Any trouble finding us?

LESLIE. *(Off)* No, no. Your directions were very precise.

ELAINE. *(Off)* And you! Look at you! *(They enter, first ELAINE, LESLIE, 39, CINDA, 11, and finally WENDY)* You're so tan. I don't think I've ever seen you so tan.

LESLIE. Well, you know that California sun.

(LESLIE is a very attractive woman who would pass for 32 but is actually older than ELAINE. Beautifully but casually dressed, her tan good looks appear almost unnaturally dark. She has a certain world weariness which makes a striking contrast to ELAINE's homespun earthiness.)

ELAINE. Here, give me your bag and let me show you your room.

LESLIE. Oh, let's just sit in here for a minute, do you mind? I'm dead from that flight.

ELAINE. Oh, sure, sure. Would you like something to drink? Iced tea? Lemonade?

LESLIE. *(Sitting on sofa)* Do you have Perrier? Or any kind of sparkling water, really.

WHERE THE TRUTH LIES

ELAINE. How about club soda?

LESLIE. Great.

ELAINE. Wendy, go get your aunt a glass of club soda, will you? And how about you, Cinda?

CINDA. Lemonade.

WENDY. Come help me.

(WENDY and CINDA exit to kitchen. LESLIE sits back on the couch exhaustedly.)

ELAINE. Rough flight, huh?

LESLIE. Oh, not so bad, really. Just, I don't know, long or something. *(Rallying)* What a pretty house! The pictures really didn't do it justice. It's so you, Elaine.

ELAINE. Oh. it's really not. If I had my druthers, we'd live in something much less gloomy.

LESLIE. It's not gloomy. It's cozy.

ELAINE. Dan likes it. All this dark wood. He thinks it's erudite or something. If he had his way, there'd be red leather club chairs and spittoons.

LESLIE. Well, I think you've done nice things with it. *(Frowning)* That stained glass window, though ...

ELAINE. I was wondering if you'd remember that. We had it in our house, remember?

LESLIE. God, yes.

ELAINE. Mother was so proud of it, I just had to have it after she died. Isn't it beautiful? Doesn't it just take you back?

LESLIE. *(Massaging her temple)* Mmm. How's Dan?

ELAINE. Oh, he's fine. He's in the guest house, writing. I'd call him in, but –

LESLIE. Oh, no, don't disturb him. The artist at work.

ELAINE. But where on earth is Missy? You haven't seen her yet. *(She goes to the foot of the stairs)* Melissa! For heaven's sake, come downstairs!

MELISSA. *(Off)* Just a *sec*, I'm on the phone!

ELAINE. Oh, God. I could wring her neck. I told her you were here.

LESLIE. Elaine, relax, I'll see her soon enough. Come sit down. It's been ages. *(ELAINE does, and LESLIE takes her hand)* I can't believe how long it's been. You look wonderful.

ELAINE. No, I don't. I look old. I'm putting on weight. No one would believe I'm younger than you.

LESLIE. Of course they would.

ELAINE. Oh, please.

LESLIE. Elaine, you look just right. Just seeing you here, in this cozy house, where you fit in so well, it's very good for me. Renews my faith.

ELAINE. In what?

LESLIE. I don't know. Life. The possibilities of life.

ELAINE. Oh, come on. You've had every possibility handed to you on a silver platter. How could my dumb little life –

LESLIE. Your life isn't dumb, Elaine. And I wish you'd stop with this silver platter stuff. It's really annoying.

ELAINE. Okay, okay, I'm sorry. *(Pause)* Look at us, you're here two minutes and we're already bickering. Don't listen to me. You know I'm just jealous of you. *(LESLIE laughs)* What?

LESLIE. Nothing.

ELAINE. Something funny?

LESLIE. No, no. Sorry. Lately I find that I'm laughing and I'm not sure why. Sometimes I look in the mirror and watch myself doing it. Have you ever watched yourself laugh?

ELAINE. I don't think so.

LESLIE. Don't. It's very depressing. *(She opens her bag)* Do you mind if I smoke?

ELAINE. Uh, well ...

LESLIE. I won't if you don't want me to.

ELAINE. I didn't know you smoked.

LESLIE. You haven't seen me in three years.

ELAINE. But you never used to smoke.

LESLIE. Listen, if you don't want me to, just say so.

ELAINE. No, no, it's just ...

LESLIE. Elaine, yes or no

ELAINE. Of course. Of course you can smoke. What am I going to do, make you step outside?

LESLIE. If you don't want me to smoke in here, yes.

ELAINE. No, I do. In fact, here, here's a ... *(She looks around the room, sees the little bowl with potpourri in it, empties it out)* Here's an ashtray.

LESLIE. That's not an ashtray.

ELAINE. Yes, it is.

LESLIE. It is not.

ELAINE. Leslie, it's an ashtray. Trust me. *(LESLIE shrugs and opens her bag. ELAINE watches uneasily as she lights up)* So how's Vic?

LESLIE. Great, great. Fine. His show is number three now, you know.

ELAINE. Number three?

LESLIE. In the ratings. "The Huntsman".

ELAINE. Oh! That's great. We watch it all the time, the girls and I. They're so thrilled to have a celebrity in the family. When he won that People's Choice award, you should have seen all the whooping and hollering. You must have been so proud.

LESLIE. I was.

ELAINE. *(Starting to gush)* I loved the way he leaned over and kissed you before he went up to get the award. And then – did you know this? I'll bet you didn't – the camera cut back to you while he was accepting, and Leslie, you looked so beautiful. Your eyes were just welling up with pride. It was like a totally honest moment captured on camera. And then when he looked at you and said, "But most of all I'd like to thank –"

LESLIE. *(Sharply)* Elaine, stop it.

ELAINE. – What?

LESLIE. Just ... don't give me your homespun Walton Family version of the totally honest moment you witnessed on TV. I just can't take it right now. Okay?

ELAINE. *(Pause)* What's the matter?

LESLIE. Nothing. It's just ... this naiveté of yours. Is it real? Or are you just cooking this up to make yourself sound like some kind of Snow White character?

ELAINE. *(Wounded)* I don't know what you're talking about.

LESLIE. Oh, come on. You think we didn't know there were cameras on us? You think we forgot that thirty million people happened to be turning in for that moment? It was a photo opportunity, sweetie. We took advantage of the moment.

ELAINE. Oh. Well, excuse me for having been touched by your performance. I won't be so foolish again.

(There is a silence.)

WHERE THE TRUTH LIES 13

LESLIE. Oh God, Lainie, I'm sorry. I'm glad you were touched. And I was very, very happy when Vic got that award. That night was so ... beautiful. Just like a dream come true.

(She turns away.)

ELAINE. Of course it was. I mean, look at you. You're crying about it even now.

(LESLIE turns back to her. She is laughing.)

LESLIE. I'm sorry. I don't know why everything strikes me so funny these days ... It just does.

(ELAINE looks at her in confusion. MELISSA comes down the stairs. She is 15 and very pretty in a way more reminiscent of her aunt than her mother.)

MELISSA. Hi, Aunt Leslie!
LESLIE. *(Still laughing)* Missy!
MELISSA. *(Coming down to meet her)* What's so funny?
LESLIE. Oh, your mother. She just always cracks me up.
MELISSA. Oh, yeah. Mom's a million laughs.

LESLIE. *(Hugging her)* Let me look at you! Missy, you are turning into a real beauty. Has anyone told you that recently?

ELAINE. *Everyone* tells her that all the time. She takes after you.

LESLIE. Oh, no she doesn't. She has her mother written all over her. *(MELISSA grimaces)* You do! How are you, baby?

MELISSA. Good, I guess. You're so tan.

LESLIE. I know, I know, it's bad for you but I just can't resist.

MELISSA. I wouldn't either, if I lived out there.

LESLIE. When are you going to come out and visit again?

MELISSA. I wanted to come last summer but Mom wouldn't let me.

ELAINE. You were there the summer before. You don't want to wear out your welcome. And anyway, it's Wendy's turn next.

LESLIE. Maybe you can both come!

MELISSA. When?

LESLIE. *(Suddenly vague)* Uh, well ... some time. Things are pretty hectic right now for Vic.

MELISSA. There was an article on him in Esquire, did you see it? He looked so handsome. My friends are ready to die that he's my uncle. And that article in People was so cool. You looked great, Leslie.

ELAINE. *Aunt* Leslie, Melissa.

LESLIE. Oh, please, I've been trying to break her of that habit for ages.

MELISSA. All my friends think you're a total babe. They can't believe your life.

LESLIE. Sometimes I can't believe it, either.

(WENDY and CINDA come back from the kitchen. They each have a lemonade. WENDY hands LESLIE a glass of soda water.)

WENDY. How come it's so smoky in here? Pee-yuu.

WHERE THE TRUTH LIES 15

ELAINE. Your Aunt Leslie is having a cigarette.

WENDY. *(Incredulous)* And you're letting her? Dad's gonna hit the roof.

LESLIE. *(Putting out her cigarette)* Lainie, why didn't you tell me?

ELAINE. Oh, it's no big deal. Dan won't be out of his office for hours.

CINDA. Here's your soda water, Mom.

LESLIE. Thanks, baby. Just what I needed.

CINDA. Are you going to eat?

ELAINE. Oh, I've got tons of food in the fridge! You could have a meatloaf sandwich, or if you want something more desserty –

LESLIE. No. Thanks, Lainie. I'm fine.

WENDY. Guess what! Cinda met Curt Cobain before he killed himself. Met him! Backstage.

ELAINE. Someone killed himself?

CINDA. He had to. He was in pain.

ELAINE. Oh, dear. That must have been upsetting.

CINDA. Not for him. It was his only way out. Suicide has a bad rep, but in other cultures it's a totally cool way to express yourself.

ELAINE. Ah. *(Pause)* You taking any sports at school, Cinda? Wendy's playing field hockey, and she's just wild about it.

WENDY. I am not, it's stupid.

CINDA. Sports don't interest me.

LESLIE. We play tennis, don't we, honey?

CINDA. You don't.

LESLIE. Well, I used to. *(To ELAINE)* I injured my wrist, so Cinda's lost her tennis partner.

ELAINE. Oh, too bad. Nothing serious?

LESLIE. No, no.

WENDY. And Cinda has her own horse!

LESLIE. We keep him stabled over at our neighbor's, but Cinda doesn't seem all that interested in riding lately.

WENDY. I would. I would ride it every day.

CINDA. You think you would, but you wouldn't.

LESLIE. What does it take to get a kid excited these days? Their own helicopter?

WENDY. I'd take the horse!

LESLIE. Wendy, you're a breath of fresh air.

ELAINE. And you are looking just wonderful, Cinda. We're so happy you're here.

CINDA. Thank you.

ELAINE. Wendy, why don't you show Cinda to your room, and you girls can get settled in. Would you like the top or bottom bunk, Cinda?

CINDA. Whatever.

WENDY. We'll flip for it! Come on, Cinda.

(CINDA picks up her overnight bag and they go upstairs.)

ELAINE. My! She's gotten very ... sophisticated.

LESLIE. Mmm. They grow up so fast.

ELAINE. You'd never guess she and Wendy were the same age.

MELISSA. *(To LESLIE)* How come Vic didn't come out here with you?

ELAINE. *Uncle* V –

LESLIE. He's shooting. And they're doing a lot of locations this season, now that the show's a hit. But he sends his love.

WHERE THE TRUTH LIES

MELISSA. Maybe I can come out some time and watch him shoot.
LESLIE. Well, sure.

(The doorbell rings.)

MELISSA. That's Chris and Mimi. I asked them over to meet Leslie. They are gonna just die.
LESLIE. *(Alarmed)* Oh look, honey, I'm not really in the mood to meet anyone right now.
MELISSA. Oh, just for a sec. They completely don't believe me that I'm related to a –
ELAINE. Melissa, your aunt said no.
MELISSA. Yeah, but just let them pop their head in and say hi. They have a total crush on Vic, and they saw the thing in People. When they see you in the flesh, they will absolutely –
LESLIE. *(Very pale, getting up)* Excuse me a minute.
ELAINE. Leslie, are you okay?
LESLIE. I'm not feeling too well. Maybe it was the flight. Is there a bathroom down here?
ELAINE. Right through that door.
LESLIE. I'll be right back. Missy, I'm sorry, honey. I'm just not ... up to it.

(She exits. ELAINE half follows, then turns back to MELISSA accusingly.)

MELISSA. Well, God, how was I supposed to know?
ELAINE. She told you no. *I* told you no.
MELISSA. Okay, so sue me! So I'm a totally evil person!

WHERE THE TRUTH LIES

(The doorbell rings again.)

ELAINE. You can just tell them to go home. Now.

(MELISSA steps outside. We hear her conferring with a couple of girls. Then she comes back in, slams the door and runs upstairs.)

MELISSA. There! You happy?

ELAINE. Melissa, you know better than to slam that door! That's antique stained glass! *(No response. ELAINE sighs, goes over to the sofa and sits down. She sees LESLIE's purse sitting on the sofa, hesitates a moment, then goes to it. With a look toward the bathroom door, she flips the clasp and looks inside. She pulls out a bottle of pills and is about to examine them when the toilet flushes. ELAINE pushes the flap back without managing to fasten the clasp, then sits back in an attempt at a relaxed position. LESLIE re-enters)* Leslie, are you all right?

LESLIE. I'm fine. I just ... that flight took a lot out of me. Where's Missy?

ELAINE. She went upstairs.

LESLIE. I'm sorry to disappoint her. I'm just not really feeling in tip top shape, and –

ELAINE. Don't apologize, please. Melissa – well, I guess she's going through a phase or something. I don't know what it is, but I can't wait for her to get over it.

LESLIE. She will, she will. We all do, eventually.

ELAINE. Leslie ... *(She hesitates)* you know I'm just thrilled beyond words that you've come out here to visit us. I've been trying to get you out here for so long I had

WHERE THE TRUTH LIES

completely given up hope. But, I've got to admit I was surprised when you said you were coming out on such short notice. I mean, twenty four hours, really, and I'm kind of wondering –

LESLIE. Lainie, if this is an imposition, tell me. We can leave, I can find a hotel, or –

ELAINE. No, no. See, I knew you'd misunderstand. I'm just trying to figure out – I mean, why now? Why after all this time did you decide to come to Vermont, of all places?

LESLIE. Why do you think, silly? Because you're here. It sure wasn't for the maple syrup.

ELAINE. But, I mean let's face it, Leslie, you've never wanted to visit before. You've been openly hostile to the idea, you said I was pressuring you.

LESLIE. Well, you were. But once you stopped begging me to come out for every Christmas, Thanksgiving, and Flag Day, I started to think, "Hmm, maybe it's time I visited Lainie." See, this is what happens when you stop nagging me. And you know what? I'm really glad I came. Because now that I see how beautiful it is, I'm thinking it might be a good idea to buy some property out here.

ELAINE. Really?

LESLIE. Sure. A summer home, maybe. You could help me look for it.

ELAINE. Oh, Leslie! That would be so exciting. You know, I've always thought it was so sad that our girls never really got to know each other. I mean, Wendy and Cinda are so close in age. And some families – you know, I have a friend, and her entire family lives within a twelve block radius of each other. Her parents, brothers, sisters, all their kids. It's like a built in support network of all these happy people. Whenever one of them gets sick, the others are right there, and they're on the phone to each other every day come rain or –

LESLIE. Elaine. I just said I was thinking about it. Let's not get carried away.

ELAINE. *(Pause)* Oh, yeah. I know. I was just, you know, dreaming aloud.

LESLIE. Yeah, well it's starting to sound more like a nightmare to me, so kindly keep it to yourself.

(There is a tense silence.)

ELAINE. Sometimes I really think you don't like me, Leslie.

LESLIE. *(Wearily)* Oh, Lainie.

ELAINE. No, you can protest all you want. But the way you treat me, the things you say to me, it's like you really hate me some times.

LESLIE. It's not true. You know it's not true. You're my sister.

ELAINE. So what? That doesn't seem to carry much water with you. It never has. I'm the one who's always sending the birthday cards and the anniversary cards and the little presents to my goddaughter. Have you ever sent Missy so much as a – *(Stopping herself)* I'm sorry, I don't know what's wrong with me. I'm so excited that you're here, and I'm acting like a total shrew. Let's start over, what do you say? Let's just pretend we haven't said a word to each other until now, and start completely fresh, what do you say?

LESLIE. That sounds fine to me.

WHERE THE TRUTH LIES

(The back door slams. From the kitchen door appears ELAINE's husband, DAN, 40. He is an intense looking man, with his mind frequently on something other than the conversation at hand.)

ELAINE. Dan! Guess who's here?

DAN. What? Oh. Hello, Leslie. Good to see you again. How long has it been?

LESLIE. Mother's funeral, I guess. Three years.

DAN. That long. Isn't that something. Here for a little vacation?

LESLIE. Yeah, a little r & r. You know.

DAN. Well, good to have you. How's Vic?

LESLIE. Oh, he's fine. Sends his regards.

DAN. Good, good. Well, California seems to agree with you. You're looking ... *(He stops)* what's wrong with your face?

LESLIE. I ... what?

DAN. Your face? Why is it that color?

LESLIE. I ... well, I have a tan.

DAN. No, no, no. What is that, a bruise? How did you get that bruise?

ELAINE. What bruise?

LESLIE. There's no bruise. Oh, I know, it's that damn blusher I bought. You have to be so careful how you put that stuff on ...

DAN. That's a bruise. Look at that. What did you do to yourself?

ELAINE. Leslie, that is a bruise.

LESLIE. *(Pause)* Boy, you don't allow a girl any dignity, do you? Okay, it's a bruise.

ELAINE. How did it happen?

LESLIE. Well, if you must know, it's one of the reasons I'm out here. I had a little plastic surgery. Just an eye lift, nothing big, and it takes a couple of weeks to heal, so I thought rather than walk around the streets of Beverly Hills looking like a vampire – you know, women do that, I've seen them, they parade around displaying their scars like status symbols – I figured rather than do that I'd escape the glare and come out here. Okay? I'm busted. Boy, you two are like a couple of detectives, you know that?

ELAINE. And so ... I mean, did they prescribe you something to take for that? You know, some kind of pill for the pain or something?

(LESLIE turns and sees her purse on the sofa, the top flap unsnapped.)

LESLIE. Why, Lainie Wilkerson.

ELAINE. I was just so worried, Leslie. You came in here looking so tired and ... and acting so strange.

LESLIE. You are a little detective. Yes, okay, they did. God! I feel like I'm getting the third degree here.

ELAINE. Oh, Leslie, I'm so relieved. You have no idea the kind of things I was thinking.

LESLIE. Well, stop thinking them, silly girl. *(She gives her a hug. To DAN)* Your wife is such a worrier.

DAN. How come you're only bruised on one side?

LESLIE. Well, you know. One side always tends to heal faster than the other. It's been awhile since I've had the surgery.

DAN. How long?

WHERE THE TRUTH LIES 23

LESLIE. Oh, gosh, it must have been – *(Pause)* a week.
DAN. Uh-huh. *(Longer pause)* You bring Cinda?
LESLIE. Sure, sure. She and Wendy are off somewhere.
DAN. Good.
ELAINE. Were you looking for something, Dan?
DAN. My atlas. It was in my office, and now it's –
ELAINE. Oh, I gave it to Wendy for her geography homework.
DAN. Elaine, I thought we agreed that my reference books were –
ELAINE. I know. You're right. It's my fault, I let her use it and then forgot.
DAN. Do you have any idea of how annoying this is? Obviously not, or you wouldn't keep giving my books away.
ELAINE. Oh for goodness sake, don't be so dramatic. I didn't give it away, I loaned it.
DAN. Lent it.
ELAINE. What?
DAN. *Lent* it.
ELAINE. *(Pause)* Excuse me. Lent it. And now I'll get it back. *(At foot of stairs)* Wendy? *(No answer)* I'll run up and get it.

(She goes upstairs. A pause.)

Dan. Do I smell smoke?
LESLIE. I don't think so.
DAN. Are you sure? I'm very allergic to cigarette smoke.
LESLIE. Oh, cigarette smoke. Well, yes, I did light up a cigarette, but Lainie made me put it out right away. Sorry.
DAN. I didn't know you smoked. *(He goes to a window and opens it)* Do you mind?

LESLIE. No, not at all. A little fresh air would be good. I smoked like a chimney in my reckless, wild, self-destructive youth, but I quit. Now I seem to have taken it up again.

DAN. Why?

LESLIE. Oh, I don't know. Nostalgia.

DAN. You going to be with us long?

LESLIE. I was thinking of moving in. That guest house of yours sounds pretty good. Just kidding. Were you worried?

DAN. *(Smiling)* You wouldn't like it out here, anyway. Not much of a fast lane.

LESLIE. You imagine my life as some kind of constant orgy?

DAN. I don't believe I've ever tried to imagine your life.

LESLIE. That's a bit rude.

DAN. Why? Do you try to imagine mine?

LESLIE. *(Pause)* Good point. I appreciate the way you never mince words, Dan, it's very compelling. I say this at the risk of sounding like I'm coming on to you.

DAN. I won't leap to any conclusions.

LESLIE. Truth is, I've always been attracted to the strong silent type. And by attracted, in your case I mean –

DAN. You don't need to explain.

LESLIE. How refreshing. I don't know why, it seems like I'm always being misunderstood. You and Elaine seem to have such a forthright relationship. No ambiguities. It must be wonderful.

DAN. It is what it is.

LESLIE. See? That kind of talk. I love it. The way you always –

DAN. You in some kind of trouble?

LESLIE. Trouble?

WHERE THE TRUTH LIES

DAN. *(Pause)* I'd better get back to work.
LESLIE. No, no trouble. Everything's fine.
DAN. Glad to hear it.
LESLIE. I mean, I haven't robbed any banks, if that's what you mean.
DAN. Yeah, that's what I meant.
LESLIE. Sometimes it's just good to get away from things, you know?
DAN. So long as Cinda's okay.
LESLIE. Cinda? Of course she is.
DAN. Good. Stay as long as you want.
LESLIE. What about your atlas?
DAN. Have Elaine run it out to me.

(DAN exits. LESLIE expels a breath of air and leans back on the sofa, relishing her first moment of privacy. Then she goes to her purse, pulls out her pills and washes two down with the remains of her club soda. ELAINE re-enters.)

ELAINE. Here it is! *(To LESLIE)* Where did he go?
LESLIE. Back to his sanctuary.
ELAINE. Oh, okay, I'll take this to him. *(She starts, then pauses)* Cinda certainly has grown up, hasn't she?
LESLIE. Yes, she has.
ELAINE. Just as I reached Wendy's door I overheard Cinda telling her she was thinking about getting a gun. She said all the kids at her school had them.
LESLIE. Oh, she's just trying to impress Wendy.
ELAINE. *(Relieved)* Oh.
LESLIE. I'm sure not even half the kids at that school have guns. It's Beverly Hills, for Christ's sake.

ELAINE. *(Pause)* I'll just take this out to Dan. Do you need anything?

LESLIE. No thanks, Lainie.

ELAINE. You sure?

LESLIE. I'm sure.

ELAINE. I baked some brownies earlier. Would you like me to bring you out a brownie and a nice glass of –

LESLIE. No, thanks. I'm just going to close my eyes for a minute.

ELAINE. I can take you up to your room if you –

LESLIE. *(Snapping)* Lainie, stop fussing over me, for Christ's sake! *(Pause, new tone)* I'm just going to take a little cat nap, and then I want to hear all about everything. Okay?

ELAINE. Okay.

LESLIE. *(Drifting off)* I'm so excited to be here ... It's just like we're girls again, isn't it?

(ELAINE watches as LESLIE nods off almost instantly.)

ELAINE. Yes. Very similar.

(BLACK OUT)

Scene Two

(The sounds of laughter can be heard coming from the dining room. Then the door opens and ELAINE, LESLIE, the three girls and DAN enter. DAN kind of hovers around the action in a disconnected fashion, never sitting. A bored person fulfilling his obligation.)

WHERE THE TRUTH LIES

MELISSA. No way! Those people are so weird.

WENDY. I'm not kidding! That's what they said! She was dead for thirty minutes, then she came back to life.

ELAINE. Oh, come on. That's absurd. First of all, who would believe it?

WENDY. Anybody who buys that stupid paper. They'll believe anything.

ELAINE. But, what kind of person would write something like that without checking the facts?

CINDA. People do all kinds of horrible things. It's better not to think about it.

ELAINE. But ... Leslie, you weren't even sick. And suddenly they have you rising from the dead?

CINDA. They didn't care. They swarmed all over us. They were probably hoping mom *would* die, so they'd have a good story.

ELAINE. Wait a minute, when was this?

CINDA. Last spring, when she was in the hospital.

ELAINE. The hospital?

LESLIE. It was nothing. It was when I broke my wrist playing tennis. They jumped on it like it was Watergate or something.

ELAINE. Did you read about it, Dan?

DAN. Uh, no.

ELAINE. I think that's terrible. Can't you sue them or something?

LESLIE. Oh, people do from time to time. But mostly it's so outrageous, all you can do is laugh.

ELAINE. I wouldn't laugh. I would be very annoyed.

MELISSA. What does Vic think about it all?

DAN. *(Sternly)* Vic?

MELISSA. Uncle Vic.

LESLIE. Oh, he pretty much laughs it off, too. Anyway, he doesn't have much to complain about. They never say anything bad about him.

MELISSA. They'd better not.

LESLIE. He seems to have a way with the public.

MELISSA. It's called the stud factor.

ELAINE. Melissa!

MELISSA. Well, it is. He's totally handsome and cool. What are they gonna say bad?

LESLIE. Well, if he's the stud factor, then I'm the Yoko factor. It just kills half of America that Vic Camden is married. That's why they dump on me.

DAN. Saying you rose from the dead is not exactly dumping on you.

LESLIE. It is in a way. You get everybody's hopes up that I might be dead and Vic will revert to a state of bachelorhood. Then you disappoint them with a last minute reprieve. "That bitch", everyone thinks. "How dare she still be alive?"

ELAINE. This is getting very morbid. Can't we talk about something else.

MELISSA. Are you going to call Uncle Vic tonight?

WENDY. Can I talk to him?

LESLIE. He's on location. He'll probably call us.

MELISSA. What kind of car does he drive now?

DAN. *(Withdrawing)* Sorry, but I think I'm going to get back to my –

LESLIE. Sure, Dan. Sorry, I know this is boring.

DAN. No, no.

LESLIE. Of course it is. If it had been entertaining, you probably would have joined in.

ELAINE. Dan's very preoccupied with his latest –

LESLIE. Opus. Yes, I know. Well, off you go, Dan.

DAN. *(To ELAINE)* If you want me to stay ...

ELAINE. No, no. This is just girl talk. You've got better things to do.

LESLIE. Dinner was wonderful, Lainie. *(Pointedly)* Wasn't it, Dan?

DAN. Yes. Very good.

ELAINE. Thanks.

MELISSA. *(Following him)* Dad, Mr. Fulton my English teacher said he thought your new book was really good.

DAN. That's nice.

LESLIE. You've got a new book out? What's it about?

DAN. The usual stuff.

ELAINE. It's about a nineteenth century explorer and his travels up the Congo.

LESLIE. That doesn't sound like the usual stuff. Your last one was about the Holocaust, wasn't it?

DAN. Mmm.

MELISSA. This one's engorged with sex, blood, and the fulminations of a half-crazed Victorian Marquis de Sade. *(The others look at her)* Well, that's what Mr. Fulton said. He even said – you know, I told you I was writing that short story? – well, I turned it in, and he said he could see some of the Flanagan style in my writing.

DAN. *(A dry laugh)* He did, did he? Well, anyone capable of engorging a fulmination must be an excellent judge of such a thing. God! What kind of idiots do we have educating our children?

(He exits. MELISSA, wounded, goes to sit on the stairs.)

ELAINE. Don't take it personally, Missy. You know how he gets.

MELISSA. Yeah. I know.

LESLIE. This must bore the shit out of him. He's a great writer, for God's sake. I can imagine what he must think about TV stars and the whole Hollywood thing.

ELAINE. Oh, he's amazingly tolerant.

MELISSA. *(Sarcastically)* Yeah, right.

ELAINE. Well, I mean considering the hardships of his profession. I think it's probably hard for any writer who's respected but not a best seller to see all of that ... well ...

MELISSA. Money.

ELAINE. Well, yes, money, that gets flashed around in Hollywood. I mean let's face it, it's very enticing. But Dan's philosophy is this:

MELISSA. "Fuck 'em. I'd rather eat rat poison."

(LESLIE laughs.)

ELAINE. Melissa! I won't have that kind of language in this house. Just because – *(Glancing at LESLIE)* Well, don't think that you can take advantage of an unusual situation and talk any way you want to.

MELISSA. God, Mom, don't have a coronary.

LESLIE. Come on, Lainie. All the kids talk like that. Hell, we talked like that.

ELAINE. No, Leslie. *You* talked like that. I never did.

LESLIE. Well, shit, maybe you should. This may be Vermont, but it's not 1958. You are the only person I know who still says things like "Good heavens" and "My word!" Sometimes you sound like June fucking Cleaver.

WHERE THE TRUTH LIES

(The girls giggle.)

ELAINE. *(Furious)* Okay. I'll fucking use every fucking bad word in the fucking dictionary! Will that make you happy?

(A silence.)

MELISSA. Mom, on you it just doesn't sound right.

(A moment of tense silence. Then, ELAINE surprises them by bursting into laughter.)

ELAINE. It doesn't, does it? *(They all laugh together. It's the first moment of communal feeling they've had so far)* It really doesn't! *(The laughter continues, and ELAINE in her exuberance goes to hug LESLIE. LESLIE cries out in anguish)* What? Leslie, what? Did I hurt you?

LESLIE. No, no. You just don't know your own strength sometimes, Lainie.

ELAINE. But I barely touched you.

LESLIE. Hey, you're a big girl. *(To the girls)* She used to tackle me sometimes out on the lawn, just knock me down like a football player. For fun! The girl didn't know her own strength.

ELAINE. Leslie, what are you talking about? I never did that.

LESLIE. Girls, this is called selective memory.

ELAINE. I didn't. You act like I was some kind of tomboy. If anything, I was too much of a wimp.

LESLIE. Okay, Lainie, if you say so.

(She makes a little face at the girls.)

ELAINE. *(Pause)* Girls, what do you say we make up some ice cream sundaes for our guests?
WENDY & CINDA. Yes!
ELAINE. Melissa, will you oversee operations?
MELISSA. Yeah, okay. Come on, you guys.

(The two younger girls dash to the kitchen, followed by MELISSA. ELAINE turns and looks at LESLIE who, suddenly nervous, goes for her purse.)

LESLIE. God, you know what? I hate to say this, but I am dying for a cigarette. And don't tell me to have it in here, I'm persona non grata enough with Dan at the moment. So I'll just step out on the porch and – *(ELAINE takes her purse from her hands and puts it down)* Lainie, what are you doing? Look, I know you don't like me smoking, but I'm a big girl now, and –
ELAINE. Leslie, open your blouse.
LESLIE. What?
ELAINE. I said, open your blouse. *(A long pause. Then LESLIE unbuttons her blouse and peels it down from her shoulders. On her neck are fiery red welts and there are scratches on her chest. ELAINE gasps in horror)* Oh, my God! Leslie.

(Silently, LESLIE buttons her blouse back up again.)

LESLIE. Happy?
ELAINE. Who did this to you?

WHERE THE TRUTH LIES 33

LESLIE. Who do you think?

ELAINE. Well, I have absolutely no idea!

LESLIE. Then think harder.

ELAINE. Not ... not Vic? *(LESLIE doesn't respond)* Why? Why would he do such a thing?

LESLIE. Because I asked him when the car was coming back from the shop.

ELAINE. *(Complete incomprehension)* What?

LESLIE. I asked him. When the car. Was coming back from the shop.

ELAINE. But what does that ... ? Did you wreck the car?

LESLIE. No. It needed an oil change.

ELAINE. An oil change. Leslie, I don't understand.

LESLIE. No. I don't expect you to.

ELAINE. Is there ... is there some kind of horrible pressure? Is *(Wracking her brains)* Does he have a brain tumor, or – ? *(LESLIE starts to laugh again, a laugh which is becoming more and more disturbing)* Well, I don't know! I mean, Leslie, you've got to help me out here.

LESLIE. No, Lainie, you've got to help me out.

ELAINE. Of course! Anything at all. I just ... I find it so hard to understand –

LESLIE. – how "Television's Bravest Hero" could beat the shit out of his own wife? Yeah, that would surprise a lot of people, wouldn't it?

ELAINE. Does anybody know about this?

LESLIE. By anybody, you mean ... ?

ELAINE. Well, Cinda for a start. Does she know about this? Was she there?

LESLIE. Not this time, no.

ELAINE. This time? *(ELAINE sinks onto the sofa,*

overcome) Oh, God, no. Leslie, how long has this been going on?

LESLIE. I don't know. Four years. Five. Cinda's a smart little girl. She doesn't miss much. *(ELAINE starts to cry)* Elaine, please. Don't. This isn't helping.

ELAINE. I'm sorry. This is just ... so ugly. I can't manage to wrap my mind around this. *(She tries to rally)* And you never told me.

LESLIE. No.

ELAINE. Surely you told mother.

LESLIE. No.

ELAINE. No! Leslie, how could you not have told your own mother?

LESLIE. Oh, please, Elaine. If you're going to go back into fantasyland again, I'm out of here. Tell mother? What for? What would she have done?

ELAINE. Well, advise you, and –

LESLIE. You know, sometimes I think we grew up in two different families. Did mother ever once *advise* you in some critical situation that made a difference in your life?

ELAINE. *(Pause)* No.

LESLIE. Okay. Thank you.

ELAINE. But she cared. She really cared

LESLIE. Okay, yeah, fine, she cared. If she hadn't been such a doormat all her life, maybe her caring would have meant something to me.

ELAINE. This is so, so horrible. Never in a million years did I imagine –

LESLIE. No? Then what was all that third degree about my pills? What was that "You can't imagine the things I've been thinking?" *(ELAINE doesn't answer)* You knew. You just didn't know you knew.

WHERE THE TRUTH LIES

ELAINE. But ... he loves you. He talks about how much he loves you all the time. On TV, in interviews. When he got up to make that acceptance sp – *(ELAINE stops)* Oh, God. What a fool I've been. No wonder you think I'm such an idiot.

LESLIE. No, Elaine. Believe me, we've got everybody fooled. It's not just you.

ELAINE. Why do you say "we"? You're not at fault here. This man who pretends to be your loving husband is doing you physical violence.

LESLIE. He does love me, Lainie. That's the worst part.

ELAINE. How can you say that? A man who beats you doesn't love you!

LESLIE. This is going to be hard to explain, but ... this thing that Vic and I have, it's different from any relationship I've ever been in. His feelings for me are so overpowering, so intense, that sometimes he just doesn't know where to put his energy. Does that make sense?

ELAINE. For God's sake, Leslie, don't you watch TV? Don't you read the papers? This kind of thing can lead to death!

LESLIE. Oh, Lainie, don't be melodramatic.

ELAINE. Melodramatic? Look at you – You've been somebody's punching bag, and you tell me not to be melodramatic?

LESLIE. He gets frustrated. It's as though his passions can't find their way out in normal ways, so sometimes he's driven to ... finding another way. I can't help but feel some compassion for what he goes through. Yes, I do! Because I see him struggling, struggling with himself, trying to find some other way to express his emotions, but sometimes he just can't, and that's when he – I hate it, I hate it so much, but part of me almost ... *(ELAINE is looking at her in complete dismay)* Don't look at me like that.

ELAINE. I'm sorry. None of this makes sense to me.

LESLIE. Well no, of course not. Dan would never in a million years be moved to strike you.

ELAINE. Thank God! *(Pause)* What do you mean, moved? You think because Dan doesn't hit me, his feelings for me are somehow – lesser than Vic's for you?

LESLIE. Of course not.

ELAINE. No, Leslie, that is what you're saying. Listen to yourself. Dan doesn't care enough to hit me. That's what you're implying. That's just sick.

LESLIE. I knew it would be useless to try to explain.

ELAINE. No, listen, I want to understand. But some of the things you're saying ... you sound as if you almost enjoy it!

LESLIE. Oh, for Christ's sake!

ELAINE. Don't get mad. Please don't get mad, but do you provoke him in some way? You know how you used to provoke me when we were kids. You'd tease me and torment me until I was ready to lose my mind sometimes.

LESLIE. *(Overlapping)* Thanks for your hospitality, Elaine. This has really been a terrific night.

ELAINE. I'm not accusing you of anything, Leslie! I'm on your side. But Vic – well, I mean I've known Vic for years now, and he's always been the sweetest, most considerate person. It's just incredible to me that he would raise his hand to *anyone,* let alone his own –

LESLIE. Never mind! I fell down the back stairs, just like Vic says.

ELAINE. That's how he's explaining this?

LESLIE. And just like you, they all believe it. Why wouldn't they? He's Vic Camden.

ELAINE. Yes, but Leslie, you're telling them the exact same thing!

LESLIE. Oh, what's the point of telling the truth? It only get him more enraged. And afterwards he's always so horribly miserable. It would be like kicking him when he's down.

ELAINE. When *he's* down? What about you? You're the one who needs protection, Leslie, not him. I certainly hope you've reported this to the police.

LESLIE. Of course I have. Many times.

ELAINE. And? What did they do?

LESLIE. They slapped us both on the wrists and sent us home.

ELAINE. Oh, come on. Even with this newfound public awareness? All the articles on abuse –

LESLIE. Doesn't change a thing. Not as far as I can tell.

ELAINE. I can't believe that. Surely the police department –

LESLIE. Elaine, you're wearing me out.

ELAINE. I'm sorry. It just all seems so ... And Vic – does he know you're here?

LESLIE. No.

ELAINE. Where does he think you are?

LESLIE. He doesn't know.

ELAINE. Well, maybe being on location he won't notice until –

LESLIE. He's not on location. He had a meeting in Century City. I grabbed Cinda and drove to the airport.

ELAINE. Oh. Well, good. Good that he doesn't know. That gives us some time to think. *(Pause)* You know, I want to respect your privacy, Leslie, so stop me if this is a bad idea, but Dan actually wrote a book once that had spousal abuse as a kind of subplot.

LESLIE. *(Wearily)* Really.

ELAINE. And I know he didn't put his best foot forward tonight, after all he is in the middle of a new book. But I really, really think it might be helpful if we consulted him about this and asked him what he –

LESLIE. He knows.

ELAINE. What do you mean, he knows? You told him?

LESLIE. No.

ELAINE. Then how could he possibly –

LESLIE. He just does.

ELAINE. That's impossible, Leslie. First of all, Dan is far too wrapped up in his own project to notice what he's having for dinner, much less intuit the complex circumstances that lead to such a thing as –

LESLIE. Okay, have it your way. He doesn't know.

ELAINE. But what I'm thinking is, it might be a good idea to tell him. Because once he hears what's going on, I know Dan, his sense of moral outrage will kick into high gear and he'll champion your cause to the death.

LESLIE. I'm sure that won't be necessary.

ELAINE. But the thing is, we've got to present an organized front. We've got to stand firm, and protect you, and – you can stay with us. You must stay with us, for as long as it's necessary. We can fight this thing, Leslie. I really believe that. Together, the three of us can –

(The girls come back in with a tray full of sundaes.)

WENDY. Ta-da!

ELAINE. *(Back into Mom mode)* Oh, my goodness. Will you look at these ice cream sundaes? Well, bye-bye waistline is all I can say. Girls, these look beautiful. Did you make them all yourselves?

WENDY. Yep.

ELAINE. Well, I can't wait to dig into mine. Leslie, here's yours. Yum-yum. Sometimes a little thing like an ice cream sundae can just perk you right up, can't it? Put a whole new light on things. Cinda, you feel free to have seconds if you want, you're our guest. And if anybody deserves seconds, you certainly do. *(LESLIE starts to laugh again)* What? What did I say?

LESLIE. That's my sister for you. Nothing so bad it can't be fixed with an extra scoop of ice cream. You're a funny girl, Lainie.

ELAINE. *(Confused)* I'm not trying to be funny, Leslie. I'm really not. *(Pause, then brightly)* Eat up, everybody!

(BLACK OUT)

ACT II

(It is the next morning. From upstairs, "Smells Like Teen Spirit" by Nirvana is playing. A figure appears at the door, partially seen through the stained glass window. The doorbell rings. Then again. A knock at the door. No response. Finally a very heavy pounding on the door. MELISSA comes to the top of the stairs, hears the pounding, and comes downstairs.)

MELISSA. Okay, okay. Keep your shirt on, asshole. *(Going to door)* That's my mother's stained glass, she's gonna murder you if you – *(She opens the door)* Uncle Vic! *(VIC CAMDEN stands in the doorway. He is late 30s, very masculine in his good looks, with a great smile. At the moment, however, he looks very unsure of himself)* I can't believe it! Come in!

VIC. Melissa?

MELISSA. Uh-huh.

VIC. My God, I didn't recognize you.

MELISSA. I can't believe you're actually here! Leslie said you were on location shooting.

VIC. Is she here?

MELISSA. She's in town with Mom. They'll be back soon. Wow! You look great. How's the show going?

VIC. Good, good. When did Leslie get here, exactly?

MELISSA. Yesterday. We thought you were going to call last night.

VIC. You thought I was going to call?

MELISSA. Yeah. Leslie said you were on location. Where were you shooting?

VIC. Oh, uh, Utah.

MELISSA. Utah! Wow!

VIC. Sweetheart, let me ask you a question: Did Leslie seem ... okay to you?

MELISSA. She didn't really feel too good, cause the flight was long. She and mom went to the doctor today to make sure she doesn't have the flu.

VIC. When do you expect them back?

MELISSA. Pretty soon. Dad's out back, you want me to get him?

VIC. No, no. That's okay. Where's Cinda?

MELISSA. Out playing with Wendy. Everything okay, Vic? You seem kind of tense.

VIC. I am tense, honey. I'm worried about your aunt.

MELISSA. Oh, I think she'll be okay. It was probably just the flight.

VIC. *(Pause)* Yeah. Probably so. Hey, look at you! What happened to the skinny kid who used to climb our orange trees?

MELISSA. God, I had such a good time in California, it was like a dream come true.

VIC. You'll have to come back.

MELISSA. I'd love to!

VIC. How old are you now?

MELISSA. Almost sixteen.

VIC. Do people tell you you look like your Aunt Leslie?

MELISSA. Yes! All the time.

VIC. I'll bet the boys are beating a path to your door, aren't they?

WHERE THE TRUTH LIES 43

MELISSA. Oh, you know. I do okay.

(She giggles.)

VIC. What are you giggling about?

MELISSA. I don't know. I'm so glad to see you. Chris and Mimi are gonna shit a brick.

VIC. Who are Chris and Mimi?

MELISSA. My girlfriends.

VIC. Are they as pretty as you? *(MELISSA laughs)* No, they're not. I can tell by the way you're laughing. They just like to hang around you so they can fight over the boys you don't want, right?

MELISSA. No!

VIC. Look at her blush. Gimme a hug, sweetheart. I've been here five minutes, you haven't even kissed your uncle hello. *(MELISSA runs to kiss him)* Thatta girl. You miss me?

MELISSA. Sure did. We all watch "The Huntsman", Vic, even Mom.

VIC. Not your dad?

MELISSA. Oh, you know dad. If it's not Washington Week in Review.

VIC. Your dad should take a look around. I'll bet he hasn't even noticed how pretty you've become. *(The back door slams and footsteps can be heard walking through the kitchen, then DAN comes in)* Hey, speak of the devil.

DAN. Well, well. Hello, Vic. What brings you to this neck of the woods?

VIC. Break in shooting. Thought I'd drop in on my wife.

DAN. Well, good to see you, good to see you. *(They shake hands)* She know you're coming?

VIC. Nope. Figured I'd surprise her.

DAN. She'll get a kick out of that, I'm sure. Sit down, sit down. Can we get you something?

VIC. No thanks, they watered me down heavy on the flight.

DAN. Flew in from California, did you?

VIC. That's right.

DAN. How's that TV show of yours going?

VIC. Not bad.

MELISSA. Not bad? It's a huge hit! Number three this week.

DAN. Well, isn't that nice. And how's California these days?

VIC. Couldn't be much better. We've got our quakes and our riots, mudslides, brushfires. Big crime problem, and the governor's a fascist. But it's God's country, it really is. We love it. Hey, this is a great place you've got here. Real, you know? No phony baloney. How's the writing coming?

DAN. Fine.

MELISSA. Dad just published a book last month. Some of the book reviewers really liked it, right Dad?

DAN. Not that it matters.

VIC. Boy, no kidding. "The Huntsman" got grilled its first season, I'm talking "Get out your gun it's hunting season on Vic Camden", and what happens? Let me put it this way – Mattel is coming out with a Huntsman doll.

DAN. Well, good for you.

VIC. See, Melissa, your dad and I are in on a little secret. It's the public who decides what's up and what's down, and nobody else. They are the only barometer of taste we care about, right, Dan?

WHERE THE TRUTH LIES 45

DAN. Actually, that's not what I said, Vic.

VIC. Oh. Sorry. Thought you did.

MELISSA. All my friends watch "The Huntsman".

DAN. Melissa, go make me a cup of coffee, will you?

MELISSA. Now?

DAN. Yeah. Now.

MELISSA. You want one, Uncle Vic?

VIC. No thanks, sweetheart. *(She exits)* Great kid. They grow up so fast, don't they?

DAN. She's a handful.

VIC. So that new book's a hit, huh?

DAN. Melissa is given to exaggeration.

VIC. Still, this could be your big opportunity, Dan. Our next door neighbor is a novelist, just sold film rights to her latest book for 1.5 million.

DAN. Well, hey, I guess I'll do that too, then. Remind me, will you?

VIC. Sorry. I must sound like a card carrying Hollywood asshole, playing the big shot with you, of all people. Remember how desperate I was, just four years ago?

DAN. I remember.

VIC. I was all ready to blow town and go study law, for God's sake, when suddenly this Huntsman thing happened and bang! Who would have thought it would take off like this? Isn't it the craziest thing?

DAN. Pretty crazy.

VIC. It's been one incredible ride, I'll tell you. The press, the ridiculous amounts of money, it's nutty out there. And I know I'm supposed to be totally happy now. I mean, this is it, right? The Big Time. But it's funny how just as your biggest dream comes true, lookie here! Twenty five new ways to become a failure. Now you've got to live up to the public's vision of who you are. It's a huge responsibility. I mean, people are watching. All the time.

DAN. Yes, they are.

VIC. It's like now that you're a public commodity, you've got to set some kind of example. And the pressure of that is kind of terrifying. But you know who I think it's hardest on? Leslie.

DAN. How so?

VIC. Vic Camden's loving wife – that's her identity right now. For a woman with her sense of self, that's a hard thing. Four years ago we were pretty much on the same level. She'd work, I'd work, we both got our chance to shine. Now she's totally eclipsed by me. You think that's not hard?

DAN. You seem very sympathetic to her situation.

VIC. Well, sure. I'm her husband.

DAN. I suppose that's why she's had this recent surgery? To help out her self esteem?

VIC. Surgery?

DAN. That's what she told us when we asked her about the bruise on her face. Personally, it looked to me like she'd been beaten.

VIC. Oh my God.

DAN. But then I know very little about domestic abuse.

VIC. ... Hey, wait a minute, you don't think that I – ? Dan, this is me! Vic! Just because I've got this image right now of being some kind of macho adventurer –

DAN. I'm not familiar with your image, Vic. And it's really none of my business, until someone comes into my house looking like that. Then I start asking questions.

VIC. I love that woman. I'm crazy about her.

WHERE THE TRUTH LIES   47

DAN. Sometimes that's all it takes.

VIC. *(Pacing)* Oh, man. What do I do here? She'll never forgive me if I ... Listen, Dan, this is really hard for me to talk about, but Leslie has some serious problems.

DAN. What kind of problems?

VIC. Where do I start? She'll disappear. I'll go crazy looking for her, then she'll come home looking like someone worked her over with a crowbar and she won't remember a single moment of what happened. It's scary, Dan. She did it again last week. Took Cinda with her this time and vanished. I'm glad she ended up here. Sometimes we're not so lucky.

DAN. You call the police when this happens?

VIC. If she's gone long enough. I'm always hoping it will be a couple few days and she'll come right back, but sometimes it's weeks. Thing is, we can't afford to let the papers get a hold of it, they'd have a field day. They did sniff something out once – it was after one of her episodes, we actually had to put her in the hospital. But we covered pretty well, so they just made up a lot of crap.

DAN. How long has this been going on?

VIC. It's been a growing thing, over the past few years. She started retreating around the middle of the first season.

DAN. First season?

VIC. Of the show. I didn't notice at first. I was busy, you know? I mean, you plug those coins in the slot machine year after year, hoping to hit the jackpot, and when it finally does, I'm telling you, it's a major shock. It's like you almost forgot what you were playing for, you've just been on automatic for so long, and now here it is all laid out before you – you can't believe how things change, Dan.

DAN. I'm sure they do.

VIC. But Leslie – well, she was always just a little bit competitive with me, you know? And now suddenly here I am, living out her dreams. I know it'd be tough on me if the situation was reversed. So maybe three, four years ago she started taking the pills. Her therapist prescribed them, what was I supposed to do? And – this is maybe the hardest part – I'm pretty sure there have been other men. God, maybe one of them did this to her. It's making me crazy, Dan. I don't know what to do about it.

DAN. Why haven't you told us about this before? Elaine's sister, missing for weeks on end. She would want to know about that.

VIC. Listen, I've made a lot of mistakes where Leslie's concerned. I didn't want to drag her family into it, too. She'd never forgive me.

(MELISSA comes back in with coffee.)

MELISSA. You like two spoonfuls of sugar, right, Dad?

DAN. That's right. *(He takes the cup)* Didn't you say you were going to go do something with your girlfriends?

MELISSA. *(Pointedly)* No. *(To VIC)* But would it be okay if I brought them over later? Just for a minute, to meet you.

VIC. If it makes you happy, sweetheart, you can bring over the whole town. *(WENDY and CINDA come in through the front door)* Well, hey! Here she is, the light of my life.

CINDA. *(Unreadable)* Daddy.

VIC. You bet it is! And who's this big grown up girl you've been playing with?

WENDY. Uncle Vic, it's me! Wendy!

WHERE THE TRUTH LIES

VIC. Wendy? No! Cinda's cousin Wendy is a little bit of a thing.

WENDY. No, it's me. It really is. I grew!

VIC. Well, look at this. It *is* Wendy! Come and give your uncle a big kiss, honey. *(WENDY runs into his arms)* Aren't you something! You and Cinda having fun?

WENDY. Sure! I took her to the duck pond.

VIC. The duck pond! I'll bet you loved that, didn't you, sweetie?

CINDA. Uh-huh. How come you're here?

VIC. I just missed you so much I decided I had to come out. Now we can all have a vacation together. Won't that be fun?

CINDA. Does Mom know you're here?

VIC. Not yet. Maybe when she gets home we can all do something together.

CINDA. Like what?

VIC. Whatever you want. The sky's the limit.

WENDY. Disneyland! Get him to take you to Disneyland.

VIC. Oh, we've been there a million times, right Cin?

DAN. Hope you won't mind, I've got to get back to work.

VIC. Oh, sure. Listen, sorry for talking your ear off like that. I'm just real concerned about this.

DAN. Yeah. Well, if there's anything I can do.

VIC. Thanks, man. I appreciate it.

MELISSA. I'm gonna go get Chris and Mimi.

(She runs upstairs as DAN exits.)

WENDY. Uncle Vic, do you really take Cinda to rock concerts?

VIC. Rock concerts, clubs, screenings. Call me a softie, I like to show my little girl off. Let's see, our last big date was ... what was it, Cinda?

CINDA. I don't remember.

VIC. Sure you do. I introduced you to the band afterwards, remember? What were their names?

CINDA. I don't know.

VIC. Yes, you do.

CINDA. No I don't.

VIC. Well, think.

CINDA. I can't remember! Please, leave me alone!

(She starts to cry. VIC looks panicky.)

VIC. Hey, hey, it's okay! It doesn't matter.

WENDY. Geeze Cinda, it's nothing to get upset about.

VIC. *(Seeming genuinely puzzled)* Honey, what's the matter? Tell Daddy, I'll make it better, I promise.

(The door opens and LESLIE and ELAINE enter.)

LESLIE. Oh my God.

VIC. Hello, Leslie. Surprise. *(CINDA runs upstairs)* Cinda, come back here, please!

LESLIE. What did you do to her?

VIC. Nothing.

LESLIE. Like hell.

VIC. Nothing!

WENDY. She's just mad cause she can't remember her last rock concert.

ELAINE. Wendy!

LESLIE. The girl is crying her eyes out.

WENDY. Well, it's true.

VIC. Well, who's fault is that? Don't you think she's been yanked around enough for one lifetime?

LESLIE. Yes! I do.

VIC. Leslie, I'm taking you home.

ELAINE. I can assure you, Vic, that is one thing you are not going to do.

VIC. Excuse me, Elaine, but I don't believe this is any of your business. Leslie? Are you coming? *(LESLIE stares at him a moment, then she turns and runs out the door)* Leslie!

(He goes to the door. ELAINE tries to stop him.)

ELAINE. Vic, stop! No!

VIC. What are you doing? Let me go.

ELAINE. Leave her alone, can't you?

VIC. What are you talking about? She's my wife! *(SOUND of the car starting)* Leslie! *(To ELAINE)* Whose car is that?

ELAINE. It's hers. She rented it.

VIC. Leslie!

ELAINE. *(Trying to restrain him)* Vic! Haven't you done enough? *(VIC breaks away and runs outside)* Vic! Don't!

(SOUND of another car starting, and careening out the driveway. WENDY has run to the window.)

WENDY. Cool! A Jaguar!

(DAN enters.)

DAN. What's going on out here?

ELAINE. Oh, Dan, Vic was just here!

DAN. Yeah? So?

ELAINE. So Leslie saw him, got in her car and drove off. Then he got in his car to chase her. Oh, my God, something horrible could happen! Should we call the police?

DAN. And tell them what?

ELAINE. And tell them – *(She looks over to WENDY)* – uh ... Wendy, why don't you go upstairs and talk to Cinda.

WENDY. What should I say?

ELAINE. I don't know, anything! Go up there and cheer her up.

WENDY. I can't. She's no fun any more.

ELAINE. Then go outside and play, please.

WENDY. I'll watch out for Uncle Vic and Aunt Leslie.

ELAINE. Fine. *(WENDY goes outside)* Dan, we've got to call the police. We can't let Vic catch up with her.

DAN. Why is that?

ELAINE. Because he's dangerous. Do you know what that bruise is on Leslie's face? *(Pause)* Vic has been beating her.

DAN. Well, somebody sure is.

ELAINE. She says it's Vic.

DAN. Okay.

ELAINE. What do you mean, okay?

DAN. Okay, I believe she's saying that.

ELAINE. What, you don't believe her? Leslie wouldn't lie, Dan. *(Pause)* She wouldn't!

DAN. Okay.

ELAINE. What?

DAN. Nothing. Just, all the stories you've told me about her ...

WHERE THE TRUTH LIES 53

ELAINE. Oh for goodness sake, that was when she was a little girl. And, okay, a teen-ager. But she's grown up now. She has no reason to lie about a thing like this.

DAN. We don't know that.

ELAINE. I can't believe you! The woman is being victimized, and you blame it on her.

DAN. I'm not blaming anyone.

ELAINE. Yes, you are. You're suggesting she's lying. Vic Camden is such a swell guy, how could he possibly do something as cowardly as beat his own wife? Why, didn't we just see him on TV the other night saving mankind? You men stick together on everything.

DAN. I wish you could hear how ridiculous you sound.

ELAINE. Oh, fine, attack me.

DAN. I'm not attacking you. You know what I think of the guy.

ELAINE. You think he's an idiot.

DAN. Not an idiot. Just limited. Seriously limited.

ELAINE. Do you think he's capable of having beaten her up?

DAN. *(Pause)* I don't know.

ELAINE. Why not?

DAN. Well, come on, Elaine. We've known him for years, long before he entered this celebrity phase.

ELAINE. Maybe he's changed.

DAN. Maybe she has. Tell me the truth, were you more than a little surprised to hear her say Vic did this to her?

ELAINE. Oh, what difference does that make?

DAN. Elaine, if you don't intend to discuss this rationally –

ELAINE. All right, all right. Yes. I was surprised. It seemed unlike him.

DAN. Well, all I'm saying is factor that in. Have you talked to Cinda?
ELAINE. Leslie says Cinda hasn't really seen anything.
DAN. How likely is that?

(ELAINE thinks about this. Then she goes to the foot of the stairs.)

ELAINE. Cinda! Cinda! Would you come down here for a moment?

(A pause. Then CINDA appears at the top of the stairs.)

CINDA. I'm sorry.
ELAINE. For what, sweetie?
CINDA. I don't know.
ELAINE. Would you mind coming down a second, Cinda? Your uncle and I want to talk to you. *(Slowly, CINDA descends the stairs)* Honey, we just want to ask you a question or two, okay? *(CINDA nods)* We're just a little worried about your mom and dad, and we're wondering if there's anything you want to tell us?
CINDA. Like what?
DAN. Like, if there's something that's making you unhappy and you'd like to share it with us. Is there anything?
CINDA. No. Everything's fine.
ELAINE. Do your mom and dad get along okay these days?
CINDA. Oh, sure.
DAN. No arguments? No disagreements?
CINDA. Everybody disagrees from time to time. That's only normal.

WHERE THE TRUTH LIES 55

ELAINE. Of course, of course. But, we're just curious, honey – how did your mom get that bruise on her face?

CINDA. *(Pause)* Do you know, I don't remember.

DAN. Maybe somebody hit her?

CINDA. Hit her? No, no one hit her.

ELAINE. Was it an accident?

CINDA. No. Well, maybe. I really don't know. May I go upstairs now?

ELAINE. *(Pause)* Sure, honey. Thanks.

(CINDA starts up the stairs, then stops.)

CINDA. You know what I think?

ELAINE. What, sweetie?

CINDA. You know how scientists keep finding out that the universe is bigger and bigger? And you know how these other scientists keep finding stuff that's smaller and smaller? I think one day they're all gonna be looking in their telescopes and their microscopes and all of a sudden realize that the absolute smallest thing and the absolute biggest thing? Is the same thing. And then everybody is going to go crazy.

(ELAINE and DAN look at each other.)

ELAINE. Hmm. Well, maybe that's true. I never thought about it.

CINDA. I'm sorry.

ELAINE. Nothing to be sorry about, Cinda. You're a great kid and your uncle and I love you very much.

(CINDA goes upstairs.)

DAN. That's one weird little kid.

ELAINE. You'd be weird, too, if you had to live the life she does.

DAN. What shitty deal of the hand assigned her those two lunatics?

ELAINE. Oh, now they're both lunatics?

DAN. I see a kid that messed up, and I think I can safely say that yes, both parents are to blame.

ELAINE. Dan, please. Will you just for one second give Leslie the benefit of the doubt?

DAN. Your problem, Elaine, is that you don't know how to think logically. You let emotion sway your every judgment.

ELAINE. I can't tell you how much I hate it when you begin a sentence, "Your problem, Elaine" ...

DAN. Here we go again.

ELAINE. Well, forgive me for being a little upset that my sister has just been beaten within an inch of her life! If you'd seen the welts on her neck and her chest –

DAN. Okay, look, I'm sorry. You have every right to be upset.

ELAINE. We should be calling the police.

DAN. And tell them what? A man has just gone off in pursuit of his wife? We have no proof that he's going to hurt her. Once they hear who he is they'll probably ask for autographs. All we can do is wait for them to come back. And you've got to try not to let your emotions color your thinking so much, will you? It will help you understand what's going on here.

ELAINE. Do you understand?

DAN. I thought I did at first, when I saw Leslie yesterday.

WHERE THE TRUTH LIES 57

ELAINE. You did? That's funny. Leslie said you did.

DAN. But then I talked to Vic before you got here, and now I'm not so sure.

ELAINE. Why? What did he say?

DAN. Well, you're not going to like it.

ELAINE. What? Tell me.

DAN. He said that she's been running away from the house for a long time now for weeks on end, and coming back all battered and bruised. He says she has a drug problem or something –

ELAINE. Oh, that is just absurd!

DAN. And that she's emotionally disturbed.

ELAINE. *She's* emotionally disturbed? If that isn't the pot calling the kettle black!

DAN. Why does that sound any crazier than Leslie's version of the story?

ELAINE. Because I know my sister. Okay, I'll admit Leslie has always been, well, a free spirit. Maybe even a little wild, from time to time. But she is not a victim kind of person, and she wouldn't go out and put herself in a victim situation. If anything, she was the aggressor when we were growing up. She could make me do just about anything.

DAN. Excuse me. Which side of the question are you arguing at the moment?

ELAINE. My point is there is no way she would run out into the night, high on drugs, and let some low lives beat her up for two weeks.

DAN. You're saying she'd prefer to be beaten in the privacy of her own home?

ELAINE. I'm saying she didn't want to be beaten at all! But that she somehow got into a situation with Vic where this violent side of his nature has come out, and she doesn't know what to do about it.

DAN. Okay, assuming that is true, why didn't she take action a long time ago?

ELAINE. Because she loves him! Because the man she fell in love with is not the man who is beating her, and she's still in love with that first man and hoping he'll come back.

DAN. Sorry. That doesn't make any sense to me.

ELAINE. Of course it doesn't. You've never loved anybody so much that you'd —

(She stops.)

DAN. That I'd what? *(No answer)* That I'd beat them up? Or that I'd let myself be beaten up?

ELAINE. Oh, face it, Dan. There's nobody you love enough to even raise a finger for.

DAN. Where the hell is this coming from?

ELAINE. It's true. You're barely aware that the rest of us are alive. How could you possibly understand the passions involved in a situation like this?

DAN. I can't believe I'm hearing this. I work night and day trying to make enough money to keep this household afloat, but I'm not aware that any of you is here.

ELAINE. Not really, no.

DAN. Well, fine. I'll stop writing completely, how would you like that?

ELAINE. What would happen if you did? What would our life be like, I wonder? *(Pause)* We'd probably get a divorce.

DAN. That's a cheerful observation.

WHERE THE TRUTH LIES 59

ELAINE. We probably would. Because then we'd be forced to talk to each other. Do you know, I think this is the longest conversation we've had in months.

DAN. And look where it's lead us. Unemployment and divorce.

ELAINE. I see. So you're saying it's better if we just don't talk?

DAN. Elaine, you're in a highly emotional state of mind.

ELAINE. So what if I am? So sue me! *(She laughs)* Funny, I sound just like Melissa. Dying for attention from the one person who won't give it to me.

DAN. Melissa, unfortunately, is very similar in nature to your sister. Her constant clamor for attention drives people off.

ELAINE. That's just not true. She's an average girl with average needs. When those needs aren't met, they become stronger than ever. That's when a person becomes demanding, Dan. When she can't fucking get what she needs!

DAN. *(Pause)* You make me sound like some kind of gorgon.

ELAINE. There's abuse and there's abuse. Sometimes silence is the worst abuse of all. It's funny, I've been thinking about this all night, wracking my brains. What is it about our childhood that would lead Leslie to let a man treat her like this? We had the calmest, least volatile family of anyone I knew. Our mother was a sweet person, religious, kindness personified. Our father wouldn't have raised his hand to us if his life depended on it. Then I started thinking about Dad. It's true, he wouldn't raise his hand. He also wouldn't raise his voice, his eyebrows, or his interest. We bored him, Leslie and me. He couldn't be bothered to raise his voice, because basically we made so small a dent on his psyche that raising it would be unthinkable. He was gone when we got up in the morning, and he retired to his office when he got home. To do what, I never knew. Read a book? Write letters? Make phone calls? All I knew was, we were never to disturb him. On weekends, he was the man who mowed the lawn, then he went to the golf course for the rest of the day. I had no idea who he was. My response to him was to stay out of the way. To be a good girl and not make waves. Leslie's was to raise hell. Who knows? Maybe she was hoping she'd get him so mad that he'd finally do something to acknowledge her presence. Like yell at her. Or hit her. Maybe being hit was all she really wanted from him. Maybe he did hit her once, one night when she came home wildly late, drunk or tripping on acid. Maybe she said or did something that finally pushed him so far, that he was moved to hit her. *(Thoughtfully)* Moved. To hit her. And she thought, "Aha! Finally I've got his attention. Finally I exist for this man."

DAN. This is sick.

ELAINE. Yes, okay, it's sick, but it's understandable. And me, look at me. Tiptoeing around this house trying not to get in your way. Hoping you liked the meal I've prepared you, never expecting to hear you say a word about it but hoping somewhere along the way it agreed with your goddamn alimentary track. Keeping the girls out of your hair just the way my mother did with us. And getting back at you for your neglect in stupid little ways like letting Leslie smoke in the house, or giving Wendy your atlas. How pathetic. What a pathetic woman I am. At least Leslie is out in the world having a life.

DAN. You're not having a life?

WHERE THE TRUTH LIES 61

ELAINE. Does this feel like a life, what you and I have?

DAN. Yes. This is a life, Elaine. Maybe you can't see it, and I don't claim that it's the best life anybody ever had, but it is a life, and it is working. You say I neglect you. Maybe that's true. But what about you? What about the way you've neglected yourself?

ELAINE. Okay, I admit I've put on a little weight, but –

DAN. That's not what I'm talking about. For God's sake give me a little credit. When we first ... fell in love, we seemed to have so much in common. We read poetry to each other, do you remember that? We discussed books. We laughed a lot, over what I really don't remember, but we did. Do you remember how much we laughed?

ELAINE. I ... yes, I guess so.

DAN. You were very political back then, we used to talk over world events and get very passionate about it. As though it mattered, as though we were part of the world, not just observers.

ELAINE. Dan, it's very hard to keep abreast of world events when you're trying to raise two active young girls.

DAN. Okay, understood. When they were babies, they required all your time. But they're big girls now. And what has happened to that woman I knew? Where did she go?

ELAINE. Don't say "Where did she go?" like I left town or something. I'm still here.

DAN. Yes, you're still here. You watch television for hours on end. You read pulp fiction. Not my fiction, mind you. For some reason, the works of Dan Flanagan are off limits.

ELAINE. You scare me, that's why! Sadistic missionaries, the nightmares of the Holocaust dragged out for the umpteenth time – I've read the book jackets and I'm afraid of what's inside. They don't jibe with the man I married.

DAN. Then did it ever occur to you the man you married might have changed?

ELAINE. Of course it has! That's why I don't want to read them.

DAN. Then I guess that means you don't want to know me.

ELAINE. No. I want to know the man I think you are. Kind, funny, good natured. Not obsessed with cadavers and sexual perversity and blood letting.

DAN. Is that what you really think I've become?

ELAINE. A person should write about what they know, that's what you've always told me.

DAN. Elaine, writing about the Holocaust does not mean I want to go out and kill six million Jews. It might mean that I am horrified by those who did, and want to understand what it is in human nature that –

ELAINE. Why? Why understand? Isn't it bad enough that there are people like that out there? Don't you want to shield your daughters from that kind of thing instead of inviting it into the house?

DAN. God, Elaine. Listen to you.

ELAINE. What? What? If you hate me so much, why are we still together?

DAN. I don't hate you. I just wonder what has happened to your intellectual hunger.

ELAINE. I don't have time for intellectual hunger for God's sake! I'm running a household! *(Pause)* Okay, maybe I take the easy way out from time to time. It's much easier to put down "My Secret Love" and run to the market than Kafka. On the other hand, at this stage in my life, "My Secret Love" interests me more than Kafka. Or sadistic Victorians. Or the Holocaust. I can't help it. Sitcoms interest me more than Masterpiece Theatre. Does that make me a monster? No, it makes me a functioning member of society. Maybe you should look at yourself a little closer. You say you're holding this family together. Well, you could hold it together a damn sight easier if you wrote something the general public could understand. Something that could sell as a movie or even a TV movie. Go ahead and sneer. I don't understand you. No one appreciates your genius.

DAN. I didn't say that.

ELAINE. No, but it's what you're thinking. The girls and I have to put up with your contempt every time you walk into a room and witness the less-than-soul-nourishing activity we're engaged in. Maybe that's why we do it so often, at least we get a reaction.

DAN. I wish I could express to you how insulting this is.

ELAINE. Express. Express away!

DAN. You're blaming me, *me,* for the fact that you've become rampant, unthinking, unjudging consumers of the media blitz. The fact that you turn to "The Huntsman" to satisfy the inner reaches of your soul is because I don't give you enough affection.

ELAINE. Indirectly, yes.

DAN. I never heard such horseshit in my whole life.

ELAINE. We're starving, Dan. Starving for you to share some little bit of yourself with us. It breaks my heart to watch Missy trying to make contact with you over and over again, and failing each time. And Wendy – Wendy makes me despair because she's so much like me, always trying to do the right thing, and be a good girl. Sometimes I want to tell her, "There's nothing in it for you, this good girl stuff. Don't waste your time."

DAN. Elaine, you have never said anything even remotely like this to me before. How come it's suddenly so true today?

ELAINE. It was always true. I just didn't see it. Or maybe I saw it and was afraid to verbalize it.

DAN. Afraid of what? Me?

ELAINE. No. Afraid of what the truth would lead me to.

DAN. What is this? Your big exit speech? You going to kick in the doll's house and blow town?

ELAINE. Let's be honest, Dan. You're not happy, are you?

DAN. Oh for God's sake, let's not get into this. Your sister –

ELAINE. No, no, come on. You demanded of me earlier that I think rationally. I'm demanding now that you look within yourself and think about what you're really feeling. Are you happy?

DAN. What is this endless American preoccupation with being happy? The Europeans think we are a hopelessly frivolous bunch, you know. I remember a Scotsman saying to me once, "You Americans place such a high premium on happiness, it's even written into your Constitution – Why is it so important to you all? Why do you think you have some kind of God-given right to happiness?"

ELAINE. And that's your answer?

DAN. I'm answering by pointing out the frivolous nature of the question.

WHERE THE TRUTH LIES 65

ELAINE. I see. Well, thank you. You've spoken volumes.

DAN. Well, what about you? Are you happy?

ELAINE. No. I'm desperately unhappy. See, that was easy. Now you go.

DAN. Why are you desperately unhappy? Are you unfulfilled? You know, I have suggested from time to time that you get a job.

ELAINE. All right, fine, I'll go out and get a job.

DAN. Do you think that will help?

ELAINE. No.

DAN. Why?

ELAINE. Because it's too late for that. I'm not qualified for anything. Any job I get at this point is going to be along the lines of checker at the local market. I'm probably not even qualified for that.

DAN. All right. So at least we can agree that I didn't rob you of your change for a big career.

ELAINE. Why are you so willfully trying not to see what I'm getting at?

DAN. Because I know you, Elaine. A crisis happens in the household, and suddenly it has repercussions on life as we know it. It can't just be that two other people have fucked up their lives. Suddenly our lives are worthless, too. Well, I don't buy it.

ELAINE. Stop it. Stop categorizing everything I do. Things don't always fit into your neat file box. Isn't it just possible that you and I have been living lives of quiet desperation for many years now, and preferred not to look at it?

DAN. All right, maybe we have. So what? What's the alternative? You want me to go out and find a lover? Would you like to walk out that door and give it a good slam, smashing your precious stained glass window to smithereens? Then what? Then what have we got? Just for a minute, envision the alternative.

ELAINE. I ... I can't.

DAN. No. Neither can I. And so far, you haven't given me a good reason why I should have to.

ELAINE. I just ... I just can't escape this fear that, when all this is said and done, my life is utterly empty and meaningless.

DAN. Darling, that's a fear I live with every day. Who doesn't?

(There is a pause. Then the sounds of card pulling into the driveway. ELAINE and DAN look at one another. A knock at the door. Then VIC opens it. He and LESLIE stand together.)

VIC. *(Sheepish)* Hi.
ELAINE & DAN. Hi.
LESLIE. Mind if we come in?
ELAINE. No, of course not.

(They step in awkwardly. WENDY pops in from behind them.)

WENDY. They're here!

ELAINE. Yes, we know, Wendy.

WENDY. That was cool., Uncle Vic. Just like a chase scene from "The Huntsman"!

DAN. Wendy, out.

WENDY. No fair! I saw them first.

WHERE THE TRUTH LIES 67

DAN. Out. We'll call you back in later.
WENDY. What a gyp!

(She goes grudgingly back outside. The four of them stand there for a moment.)

ELAINE. Leslie, are you okay?
LESLIE. I'm fine, Lainie. I just ... we just really want to apologize to the two of you for what we've put you through in the past twenty-four hours.
VIC. It was really immature of us to drag other people into our own personal troubles, and we're sorry.
ELAINE. Don't be absurd. Something of this nature, it's only natural for –
LESLIE. Lainie, I ... you're never going to forgive me for this, but I've been kind of leading you down the primrose path a little bit.
ELAINE. What do you mean?
LESLIE. Oh, God. Well ... okay, here goes. The thing is, I was really, really mad at Vic. But not for the reason I told you.
ELAINE. No?
LESLIE. I'm sorry. You're going to hate me. But the fact is ... okay, the fact is he gave me this beautiful new Porsche for my birthday, I mean it was so pretty, Lainie, I wish you could have seen it. It was a white convertible, a 944, just beautiful. Anyway, the other night we were getting ready to leave this party, and Vic absolutely insisted on driving it home.
VIC. I really shouldn't have. I had been drinking, more than a little. I was just doing this macho "I have to drive" thing, you know?

LESLIE. It's true, he was. You're really unbearable when you get like that, you know? But I'm at fault, too, because I let him. We both took a foolish risk. Anyway, wouldn't you know he cracked it up. I got these injuries I showed you, which aren't so bad when you think about it because the car was totaled. And Elaine, I got so goddamn furious. I mean it was a brand new car, it was my birthday present, and I wanted to drive it. *(To VIC)* I told you I wanted to drive it!

VIC. I know, baby. You were right.

LESLIE. *(To ELAINE)* Well, he's being really sweet about it now, but you should have seen him that night. You'd have thought it was my fault.

VIC. Look, I'm a louse, what can I say. Men are pigs, right, Dan?

LESLIE. So I came flying out here in high dudgeon, completely furious.

VIC. Not too furious to forget to leave a note saying where you were going.

LESLIE. No, I guess not that furious. And then – I don't know what's wrong with me, I found myself making up all this horrible stuff about Vic to make him look bad. I was just so pissed off, you know? I wanted to hurt him in some way, so I told you that he did this.

VIC. Well, don't feel bad, babe, because you should have heard what I told Dan.

LESLIE. What did you tell him?

VIC. Oh, you don't want to know.

LESLIE. No, tell me!

VIC. Let's just say it wasn't very nice.

LESLIE. Oh, you are a monster, you know that? *(CINDA enters at the top of the stairs)* God, you guys, we are both just

WHERE THE TRUTH LIES

horribly embarrassed. I hope there is some way that you won't hate us forever.

ELAINE. Is this some kind of a joke?

LESLIE. A joke? No. What kind of sick person would joke about this kind of thing? *(She looks up and sees CINDA)* Oh, Cinda, there you are. Everything's okay, sweetie. Come on down here and give us a big –

(CINDA turns around and runs back into WENDY's room, slamming the door.)

VIC. Uh-oh. Looks like we're going to have to have a talk with our little girl.

LESLIE. It's terrible that we had to put her through this. I really hate myself.

VIC. It's not your fault, honey, it's mine. Believe me, I'll make it up to her.

(MELISSA comes bounding down the stairs.)

MELISSA. Wow! What was all that about? We saw you guys go zooming off.

VIC. Leslie and I had a little tiff but it's over now. Sorry, Missy Most Beautiful. Did we ruin your plans?

MELISSA. Not if you come outside and say hi to my friends.

VIC. We'd be delighted, right, honey? *(He throws an arm around MELISSA, who blushes with delight)* I cannot believe how this girl has grown. She looks just like Leslie, doesn't she?

ELAINE. *(Firmly)* It's just a stage.

VIC. We want her to come out real soon for a visit. I'm not kidding, a girl like this could go far in L.A. Have you ever thought about being an actress, pumpkin?

MELISSA. All the time!

VIC. Well, don't. Who needs the heartbreak, right, Leslie? *(LESLIE gives him a sharp look which he ignores or doesn't see)* You can do plenty in that town without subjecting yourself to the misery of the actor's life.

MELISSA. I'm so glad you guys are here. I love you both so much!

LESLIE. We love you, too, sweetie.

VIC. Come on, let's go out and see this junior press conference you're arranging. *(They start out the door) (To DAN and ELAINE)* We'll be out of your hair by tonight. And really, we're sorry for our lousy behavior. I'll make it up to you, I promise.

(He goes out with MELISSA. LESLIE lingers at the door.)

LESLIE. Lainie, I'm so embarrassed about all this I can barely speak, but I hope when all of this blows over you'll let me call you and explain the whole thing more completely. Vic is so sorry about the whole thing, you should have seen how miserable he was. He cried, Lainie. He really did, he cried like a baby. It broke my heart. And without Vic, I feel like I'm just walking in my sleep, Lainie. Like I'm this sad little sleepwalker just waiting to be waked up.

(She smiles tenderly at both of them and goes out. ELAINE and DAN are silent.)

DAN. What just happened here?

WHERE THE TRUTH LIES

ELAINE. She's lying.

DAN. They both are. *(Pause)* Aren't they?

ELAINE. Well, they'd have to be. Unless ...

DAN. *(Pause)* I don't think I've ever seen Melissa so animated.

ELAINE. She loves them. She always has. She talks about them all the time. *(Pause)* Maybe they're not lying. Is it possible they're telling the truth?

DAN. I don't know ... I've lost my grip on this whole thing. They're very convincing.

ELAINE. Well, they *are* both actors. *(Pause)* There's something very unnatural about this whole thing. *(She goes to the window)* I fear for her future, Dan, I really do. I look at them, and it's like I'm looking at tomorrow's headlines.

DAN. Well, one thing, Melissa is not going out to California.

ELAINE. Absolutely not. I can't imagine a worse influence. *(DAN joins her at the window)* Look at them out there. They look absolutely hugely happy.

DAN. Like nothing has happened.

ELAINE. I cannot believe she has done this to me. Again.

DAN. What do you mean, again?

ELAINE. This is exactly the sort of thing she would do to me as a child. Get me all riled up about something, and then suddenly just walk away, or change the rules, or act like nothing has happened. Leaving me looking like the stupid one. God, she makes me angry! I fell for it again!

DAN. Unless what she told you yesterday is the truth.

ELAINE. How are we ever going to know? The truth keeps changing with her. *(Pause)* You know who's really being victimized here?

DAN. Who?

ELAINE. Cinda. This is child abuse of the worst sort.

DAN. Oh. I thought you were going to say us.

ELAINE. Us? *(They look at one another)* Oh. Well, yes. You're right. She had no right to get me so excited. I'm sure I said a lot of things I didn't mean.

DAN. We both did. But you're absolutely right. The real victim is Cinda.

ELAINE. *(Pause)* So, what do we do now?

DAN. What do we do? You mean, you and me? *(They look at one another)* Well, do you want me to ... I mean, if you want help around the house in some way, or with dinner or something ...

ELAINE. No, no. I've got it all under control. Do you think they'll be staying for dinner?

DAN. God, I hope not.

ELAINE. It would be horribly uncomfortable.

DAN. But if they do, I'd be happy to go to the market and get some more of ... whatever it is you're cooking.

ELAINE. Do you even know where the market is?

DAN. Of course I do.

ELAINE. Sorry, sorry. That's very nice, but I'm sure you want to get back to your book. Don't you?

DAN. Well, you know, I am kind of in the middle of -- I've gotten to the place where all the loose ends are being tied up, and if I get too distracted –

ELAINE. No, don't distract yourself.

DAN. But when I'm done, if you'd like to read it ...

ELAINE. Definitely. This time I really will.

DAN. I'd welcome any critique.

ELAINE. Oh, I wouldn't do that.

WHERE THE TRUTH LIES

DAN. No, I'd appreciate it. You used to really let me have it.

ELAINE. Yes, but you were just starting out. Now ...

DAN. Nothing's changed. I'm the same old person. It's the same old stuff.

ELAINE. I'm sure that's not true.

DAN. You're not going to read it, are you?

ELAINE. Of course I am. If you want me to. Really. *(A pause. Then a cheer goes up outside. They turn to the window)* I can't get over how happy they look.

DAN. They're not happy. It's a facade.

ELAINE. They've come to a mutual agreement to sweep this whole thing under the carpet. How monumentally blind! Don't they see how much pain they have ahead of them?

DAN. At the moment, clearly not.

ELAINE. How long can something like this go on?

DAN. Who knows? Maybe they'll just keep kidding each other forever.

ELAINE. Not when people are that miserable, Dan. Eventually something has to give, don't you think?

DAN. I don't know. Maybe they think it's safer not to face the truth.

ELAINE. Safer? In their case, I would say it is decidedly more dangerous.

DAN. And yet look at them. They seem perfectly content. Excited, even. Like something about this has charged them up with new energy.

ELAINE. But we saw what they were like only half an hour ago. Those kinds of problems don't just disappear.

DAN. No, they don't.

ELAINE. It makes me sad.

DAN. Well, don't dwell on it. You know how you tend to dwell.

ELAINE. I do, don't I?

DAN. Yes, you do. You're the dwellingest creature I know.

ELAINE. Well, nobody knows me like you do.

DAN. Try to remember that from time to time, will you?

(She puts her head on his shoulder. They continue to look out the window.)

END OF PLAY

COSTUME LIST

ELAINE
ACT I:
> Blue flowered rayon dress, stockings (2 pairs), watch, earrings, silver necklace, flat shoes (beige cloth)

ACT II:
> Cotton flowered blouse (multi-color), jean skirt, repeat stockings, repeat shoes, purse (woven olive w/wooden beads), earrings, repeat watch

LESLIE
ACT I:
> "Butter" silk blouse (double), "butter" jacket w/ivory zigs, jeans, shoes (brown short boots), ivory & gold back pack, make-up welts, jewelry (earrings), necklace, watch

ACT II:
> White sweater, blue wrap-around skirt, repeat back pack, repeat shoes, repeat all jewelry

MELISSA
ACT I:
> Off white bodysuit, jean vest, green rayon skirt, white anklets, shoes (black sneakers), earrings (floral), hair, necklace (drop necklace)

ACT II:
> Blue print dress, repeat shoes & socks, jewelry (repeat)?

CINDA

ACT I:
> Ivory opalescent jacket, silk blouse (lavender), mini skirt (lavender plastic), ivory socks, shoes (ivory high heeled sneakers), necklace (purple floral)

ACT II:
> Ivory top, ivory sweater, ivory pants, repeat shoes, repeat socks, repeat jewelry

WENDY

ACT I:
> School clothes (pink striped shirt & jean overalls), socks, beige Old Navy sneakers, jewelry - necklace (silver butterfly)

ACT II:
> Play clothes (off white shirt & turquoise checkered shorts overalls), repeat socks, repeat shoes

DAN

ACT I:
> T-shirt (gray & maroon), plaid shirt (gray & green), pants (beige & navy), shoes (casual brown), watch (brown w/gold), brown belt

ACT II:
> New shirt, everything else repeats

VIC

ACT II:
> White button down shirt, jeans, jacket (butter colored), belt, black lace-up boots, watch

PROPS

Please keep in mind this is not a props list. As rehearsal and production continue, we will be adding and subtracting. Also, as always, all suggestions will be greatly appreciated.

Most items to be "Laura Ashley" - country - colonial in look and or feel.

Sofa: 6'0" x 2'6"
Chair to complement sofa
End table: 2'0" x 1'6" plus frilly table cloth
End table: 2'0" x 1'9" plus frilly table cloth
Coffee table: 3'0" x 1'6"
Small side table
Area rug: 9 x 12
Hallway runner: 2'6" x 12'0"
Area rug (oval): 3'0"
Table lamp: 18" high
Table lamp: 24" high
Antique music stand
Wall sconces: candle or hurricane lamp motif
Ceiling fixture (hallway)
Antique coat hanger: wall mounted
Cedar chest: 2'0" x 1'6"
Throw pillows
Small window shears: lace motif
Framed pictures for walls: discuss
Needle work
Wicker baskets
Copper items: pots, vats, etc...
Candle sticks

Any small antique items
Hurricane lamps
Old books
Potted plants
Old broom
Pottery collection (as much as possible)
Pewter collection (as much as possible)
Crockery
Faux fruit
Any folk-art items: weather vanes, cow images, ducks, etc...
Vases
Door hardware
Window hardware
Old tins

plus anything else we can think of.

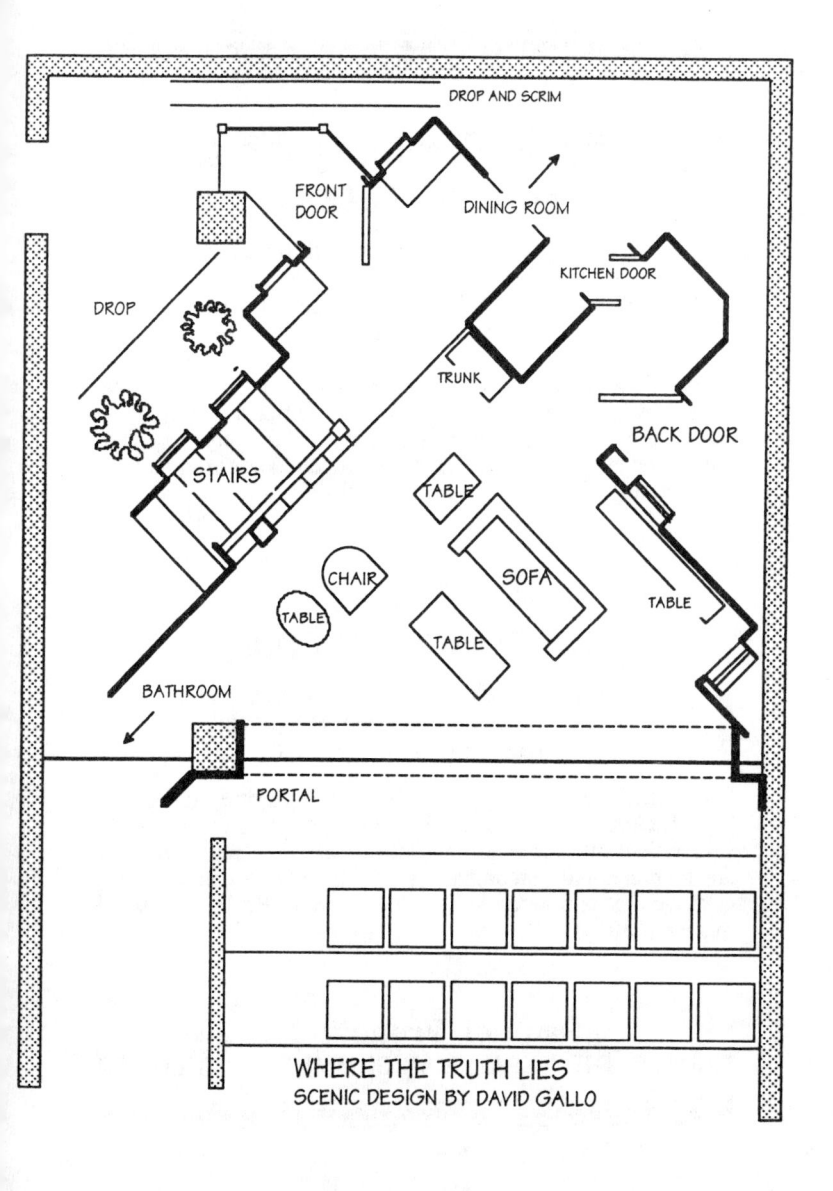

WHERE THE TRUTH LIES
SCENIC DESIGN BY DAVID GALLO

The Radical Mystique
ARTHUR LAURENTS

"Achingly earnest comedy of manners."
THE NEW YORK TIMES
"Full of caustic wit and moments of wisdom."
NEW YORK DAILY NEWS

In the New York of the late 60's when "radical chic" was coined by Tom Wolfe, friends Josie and Janice are arranging a party to benefit the Black Panthers. In the process, their complacency is shaken and they are forced to confront realities they would rather ignore. 3 m., 5 f. (#19961)

Dog Opera
CONSTANCE CONGDON

"A singular work created by an imagination of redeeming freedom and eccentricity."
THE NEW YORK TIMES

Peter and Madeline, who are now in their thirities, have been best friends since childhood. Even though they are more loving than most couples and both in search of a partner, they are fundamentally incompatible in this moving contemporary comedy that premiered at The Joseph Papp Public Theatre. 5 m., 2 f. (#3866)

Samuel French, Inc.
SERVING THE THEATRICAL COMMUNITY SINCE 1830